Golden Chrysalis

Wings for the Soul

Mary Stewart Anthony
A Collection of Poems

Photography by John Anthony

Manzanita Writers Press—Angels Camp, California

Golden Chrysalis: Wings for the Soul: A Collection of Poems

ISBN: 978-0-9968858-2-9
Library of Congress Control Number: 2017963997

Author Contact: mary.p.anthony@gmail.com
Lovesongofaflowerchild.com

Publisher: Manzanita Writers Press
PO Box 460, Angels Camp, California
manzapress.com
manzanitawp@gmail.com
209-728-6171

Book design: Joyce Dedini

Dedication

To my Irish mother
Susan McBride
Whose gift of reciting poems
Learned by heart in Ireland
The enchanted land of her childhood
Blessed my young soul
&
To lovers of poetry
In every language
Both written and spoken
Who stop and listen
As they journey on
Devoting attention
To seasons of beauty
Moments of truth
Who take us deeper
Into life's wildly beating heart

Chrysalis

The word Chrysalis comes from the Greek word, "khrusos" meaning gold, possibly of Semitic origin, Hebrew "haruz," defined as the sheltered stage of something or someone in formation.

A budding writer could not emerge
from his chrysalis too soon.
—Wm. du Bois

Photo by Ryan Bird

Naked Chrysalis

Song of the Chrysalis

When did I begin to sense
An overarching ache for change and
Stop crawling low-bellied on the earth

How did my legs find a path
Upon a slender tree to graze
Branches lush with leaves and morning dew

How strong was the pull of this erstwhile
Paradise that drew me, where I lingered
Awhile at all the feast before me

When did my pace slow down
Pleasure stopping just beyond my reach
Or my body know the end of its pursuit

How did such a bold desire
Grip me, move and wake me to cast
A silken knot to hold and hide me

How long did I dangle here before
I began the steep dark climb into myself
So I could disappear

How did such a fierce struggle spin
The liquid life out of me, shake off these
Withered legs that journeyed me here

Where I wait inside a golden vase of light
Reflecting beauty not my own—for the time
My newborn self will sail across the sky.

Dew on Azalea, Costa Rica

A Plea for Reading Poetry Aloud

Poetry must make music, or it cannot cast its spell. The ancient bards wove together words by sound and rhythm, sometimes accompanied by harp or lyre, to enhance the art of mythic storytelling.

Music reaches the heart first before meaning and sense can penetrate the conscious mind.

Poetic rhythms capture our wandering souls and open portals of fresh discovery.

Because poetry is polysemous, it may cause a fight or flight reaction in the linear mind. Poetry wants to rumble on through, overturn timetables, and upset the way we view and do life's business.

Poetry always seeks to lift the veil a little, and resurrect a sleeping soul from the labyrinths of daily life. A small flame of a poem can do it.

Learning a poem, prayer, or song by heart will engrave it on your innermost being. It becomes a spiritual treasure, a resource to call on anytime and share with others to enrich their lives.

Contents

Photographs

Monet's Garden

Through a Looking Glass

"For now we see through a glass, darkly."

1 Cor. 13:12 KJV

Big Sur from Hurricane Point

Places

Edges

Ode To Big Sur

When the earth quakes, edges blur
Or crumble, careen over cliffs
Pinned beneath the tumbling rocks
Or buried under oozing mud
Though we prefer them immutable
Or unmovable

We lean on edges like friends
Hoping they stay where they belong
When the earth bowl shifts, edges erase
Familiar borders in a moment and change
Enlarge, or shrink and disappear

Big Sur has no indelible edge
And draws no boundary
Many come and ask if what
They see is all there is
This name, written on a map
Is never fixed upon a place

The matrix is what matters
And the message that it bears—
We are guardians of these monuments you see
We are lovers of this wildness, this well of primal purity
We tend her altars and preserve her ageless beauty
We are keepers of this hearth, these mountains, and the sea

She hides a moveable feast
From the merely curious, and
Celebrates Sabbath as the emptying
Of what consumes us, before
She lifts a veil for the soul
Hungering for peace

Thirst draws us to a secret place
Where the eternal meets each true seeker
Where love heals the pain of being merely mortal
Where an edge of light dissolves the distances
Joining earth with heaven

Sanctuary

Ode to Santa Cruz

This is a pleasant land
My earthen cup of blessing
And I drink it, deeply grateful

I breathe the salted air made richer still
By ancient trees deeply rooted
Among steep hills
That lend us their pure green breath
In soldierly stands, those flame-hewn pillars
Building sanctuary here

Winds thunder out commands and
The sea must bow and break beneath
My feet, sucking sand between us, digging
Bigger holes under green rolling tides
Where tiny shells hasten to hide

Those who play and slide upon her
Arching back, will dive beneath her icy skin
Dripping with foam. Creatures leap out of her
Dip into her, skim over her, nourished
By the heaving of her shining breast

Boats float by slowly and triangular sails,
Like diaphanous veils, wave adieu
Heading out to catch the gilded sundown
We taste the cool wind that drives them
And watch like sentinels along the shore

This is seedbed growing out of goodness
Oh yes, it's fertile stuff. No goddess needed here
This is how I hear her song, wear her
Cross of lapis stone, and bring Shalom
Where I now live and shall belong

This is a pleasant land
My earthen cup of blessing
And I drink it, deeply grateful

When Haiti Descended into Hell

Rubble, concrete dust, tumbled pillars, splintered roofs
Bricks unmoored from mud, askew on twisted streets—
Scrape a landscape raw
An apocalypse of vacancies
Without mercy, in a country we call Haiti

Crushed limbs bleed and rot, as gangrene climbs up
Swollen veins and screams of buried living ones
Call out. Some mix their prayers with songs
While the slashing shovels pitch hard
Against the stone debris, slowly
Carefully digging closer to the voices

We glimpse bodies dumped for landfill
Become jumbled limbs and pieces
Children orphaned without warning
Search for familiar faces, "Auntie, cousin, uncle?"
Worried mothers carry sacks and little ones
Upon their backs, and walk uncounted miles
Before they find a waterspout

Strangers scurry to lift up
Stone from stone, to knit the bone again to flesh
To bind the gaping wounds of missing limbs
To hold the trembling hands that cannot light
A candle yet, or bear to see what lies beyond

The moaning shadows, to touch the sunken
Eyes of pain no medicine can heal
Pause to hear the anguished
Cries when a beloved name is called and
Written down among the dead

Tears become the only language we can read
When words are choked and buried under grief

We looked upon this horror as if it were our own
Stunned and shaken to the core. Some, gut-wrenched
Left their comfort zones to offer all they had to give
If only these could live

Fog on the Hills in China

Ghost Sonata

Xi'an, China

This pale ghost of Xi'an's sun can
Still fire membranes of memory

Undo them from the haunted
Spell of sleeping cells

Unbind the mind, cat-curled
In luxurious repose

Unleash it open-mouthed
Upon the tender entrails

Of this fragile newborn light
Draw the breath of wonder in

Let the eye spill over with fresh hope
Bury the dark underbelly

Of dreams squandering the night away
Sink the pearl of day deep beneath

The crevices of flesh and bone
So it will not be lost

Or your soul will count the cost

Burning the Rim of the World

A Forest Fire near Our Home in 2015

Now I bless every tree in passing
Broad vistas full of majesty
Still flourishing and flying green

Not chewed to charcoal pieces or
Choked to ashen memories
By the fire-breathing dragon

That torched the rim of our world
Extinguished into plumes of smoke
Exploding before our unbelieving eyes

Dyeing all our skies blood red, grim grey
I mourn the smoldering land where
charred stick figurines are planted

Among ghostly silhouettes on
An earth scorched to moonscape
Uprooting the forest of our dreams

We wait for drops of mercy to resurrect
To heal the buried cones of seed
Redeeming every flame that screamed

Every roar of death rattling the throats
Of living trees and gasping branches
I rage against the mushroom clouds

Floating upwards, bloated wastrels
Sucking all the precious moisture
From dry-boned soil and withered limbs

I rejoice in every beam of light
Sifting through the blackened earth
To reveal tender remnant shoots

Fighting for their right to live
I have learned the lesson of renewal
Is the burning of it all to free the soul

A Walk from Stone House Inn

Carmel, California, 1989

The heart, hungering for breadth,
Leaps out upon the ocean to find rest
And remembers how to breathe in silence

This heaving breast has calmed us
Into leaving all our expectations
And cradled all our silent questions

Many a dream has been offered here
In burning temples of the sun
Many a soul has plotted out its final run

Many a path worn by wanderers,
By trailing moons, and falling stars
Have been erased before the questing eye

Yet we glimpse in the green and icy clutch
Of waves, our fierce desire, our fervent pitch
To reach our journey's end at last

When its power is unleashed, an invisible wall
Holds it back. We dig in our feet like rocks
And defy this immensity to pass over us

Now the soul, suddenly emboldened
Thirsting still, kneels to be washed
Under stinging, salted lash, and purified

In the golden days, they used to speak of God
Brooding over churning darkness, and the void
Until a rosy skin broke open, bringing everything to birth

Many a heartbeat, like the waves' ceaseless pounding
Has been subdued under a moonbeam's balm
While awaiting the warmth of His bright wing

Sunset in Costa Rica

La Puesta Del Sol

Sunset on the Grand Canyon

The heavens swooped in feathered clouds
Above my sky-stretched mind
Like birds on fire in the soundless wind
Pluming out blue flame, and veils of rosy smoke

A drooping wing brushed against the blaze
Of light hanging just a moment more
Before the final streaks of dark-defying day
Were swallowed by the night

Sundown scorched the blackened trees
And painted languid silver lakes
Until the sky draped velvet over mountains
And icy veins vanished into steaming rocks

The canyon reared up high and glowing
Arching mesas loomed above the shadowed walls
Leaves were burning on their branches
As trees caught falling embers of the sun

Each passage of the sun has power enough
To dissolve these trees, these stones, and
Slowly change these molten monuments
Into such illuminations, and a song

Winter Camp in Yosemite

Sitting in the realm of early light
Under a tent of trees
I wait to be touched
By the gentle scepter of winter's sun.

Feeling cold limbs arch and stretch
To be warmed by this pale flame
I wait to be birthed
Out of darkness and begin once again.

Heaven's eye has burned away the night
Of primal wilderness.
I wait to be healed
By tender beauties this day reveals.

Half Dome from Glacier Point, Yosemite

Lessons from a Silk Factory in Thailand

Grace is not
A mantle falling softly down
Upon our shoulders, bowed in despair

Nor knit of silken strands, their strength
And sheen I've seen spun from the boiling

And uncoiling of cocoons that separate
The worm from all its spinning

The silent grinding out of leaves
Swallowed into gut has unwound

A thread as its final utterance
Hanging like a delicate web

Destined to become a womb
Soon defiled by death.

Grace is purely blood-borne
Running incandescent under

The skin and bone of God
Whose wounded Love has

Unwound us from the choking coils
We made, and bestowed living wings

Upon the dying worms we once were
Unlocking us from cells of doom

His fingers curl in a caress
His wings unfurl and whisper peace

Around us, choosing to bless and fill
Our helpless upturned hands

Nothing less. Grace is
The thinnest strand of light given

That we are called to walk upon
spanning a bridge to realms unknown

Between the downward pull of earth
The upward lift of heaven

Hungarian Pathway

Pilgrims

A Rebel's Iliad

I sing of angels climbing down on moonbeams
Sent here to guide us to our home among the stars

Of demons spinning webs of dread-filled dreams
Who build labyrinths to feed the jaws of death

I sing of Light unlocking chains of fear
Banishing unholy darkness to its doom

I sing of Love that sent a mighty Prince
To yield his life and break the yoke of sin

Probing deeper into the heart of things
Must be the poet's singular passion

Who plumbs the depth or measures out the air
Vibrating into breaths of spoken words?

Who writes the music for each syllable of sound?
Language, more than old Promethean fire

Is given as a boon to man, and illumines
Shadowed passages among the chambered rooms

Of every searching soul. If time moves in a line
As a dimension, and changes our perception

Of light and space, then reality will depend
On the ground of being where you stand

One day I climbed to higher ground, and traced
My steps as far as mind could bend, and found

My path unwound into a new direction
Wisdom had gleaned meaning from confusion

Patience gathered memories into boxes
Beauty polished moments buried deep in dross

It's then you suddenly realize Love has
sustained you, against all odds above the fray

Your runaway rebellious soul escaped
The stalking terrors of the night—your mind

Once held captive, poisoned, broken, raped
Had been healed by words of truth and light

Though we divine genetic coils of mysteries
Scale the spiral ladder or decode a sequence

We miss an incorruptible inheritance
Earthly life can be distilled in drops of blood

Our cells may spell out lines of health
Or point out deadly patterns of disease

Yet none predicts the purpose of existence
Or fathoms the length of all our days

It's another kind of sinkhole we've devised—
Only communion between human hearts will tell

The truest story—our difference or sameness
Will fully play each other out in time

Eternal verities are found in how we touch
Each other, skin to skin. This translucent veil

Of tissue is a pale fabric, binding us as one
When tender hearts recoil, the skin will crawl

When icy hearts melt, the skin burns. Under
This immense organ we are visible, vulnerable

It trembles with desire, shakes with fear, grows
Fluid in beauty, lunges out in brute power

Molded underneath this fragile armor
We strut about as bold as any god

Defiling the earth who is our Mother
Profaning the heavens of our Father

Proclaiming self-engendered evolution
Though we climb higher, we fall like beasts

Into a morass made of self-delusion
Pinioned by a bittersweet illusion

Dragging us to tragic depths of ignorance
No matter how high we leap or prance ahead

The remains of this brief life cannot be reduced
In labeled fragments to measure out worth

Desperate to understand the few seasons
Of my sojourning, I dug away the clods

Of clinging earth, uncovered wounds become
Cicatrizes, artifacts of my survival

Scars became signs, tender insignia held in
Membranes of memory, embedded in nerves

Like delicate fingers, touching the roots of pain
Underneath the tender shoots of joy

I culled them from their burial mound
All have been found, yet not fully uncovered

What we have spoken, stroke on stroke, written
Onto flesh and bone, can never be unwritten

You must love the Truth so much you bless
The stinging shards of light piercing deeper

Through broken bits of clay. You fit them
Piece to piece and tie up bundled twigs of time

Day by day the jumble awaits you as the sun's
Unhastening eye strips the fragments clean

Then you pause to read some forgotten name
By candlelight and remember how you prayed

The thrill of rediscovery drives all
The pistons forward until your soul joins

The backwards journey singing its song
Such a gentle moonlight draws you down

Paths hardly discernible until
You press beyond overgrown ways

Until you wander, and you linger
Under such a beauteous blur

Of worlds gone by, of worlds to come
Of worlds without end

An earlier version called, "Prologue for a Pilgrimage" published in Book One of my memoir, *Love Song of a Flower Child*, WestBow Press, 2012.

Pilgrimage

Each pilgrim carves a path of faith and
Leaves it for another who will follow

Glory is the air we breathe and cherish
For as long and deep as we are able

Grace has built this tent of earthly meeting
We all share, and will reveal us soul by soul

In this clothing we all wear, light is woven
By the One we love, yet have not seen

Love is the language learned from our Father
Teaching us to speak in truth to one another

As pilgrims we walk upon this earthly green
With care, bearing all to reach our heaven

Sunset, Domical Beach, Dominican Republic

Once and Only

Time has moved us millimeters on
Tiny motions much against our will

Learn to be content in a dimension
That must move us further still

The trail of distant images that follow
Smile from somewhere we once were

But we have vanished in the search
Nothing holds us to the core

Blood beating hard against the ear
Still binds us to this shallow perch

The slow trickle of sand cannot display
The once and only power of the day

So fill the glass of hours full
And if our final angel has not come

Mercy's hand will turn it once again
Restless in a sea of discontent, we look

Through melting mirrors and mirages
Stranding us on shores of an enigma

So soon we wanderers are mesmerized
By the shining push and pull of tides

Rising past the last horizon of our eyes
Our souls float trance-like in this tumble

Enchanted by ancient signs once visible
We gaze upon the fading map of starlight

That once charted paths between unknowns
Everything we've wrapped in a familiar skin

Will soon dissolve to mystery beneath the sun
Still we separate the bone from marrow

Hoping there's a message for tomorrow
Yet this is how we lose the way

Of knowing only what is now is
Bathed in quintessential light

Living words like flames appear
To spell our names upon the air

They illuminate our book of hours
Bound with treasured memories

Those passages within, when as a child
Eternity once opened like a flower

Time will soon wither and bend
Beneath its own weight of tyranny

Crushed underfoot by death and be
No more our mortal lord

Then a kingdom on a sea of glass
In a globe of light will descend

To unfold an inheritance of grace
A place Love promised and prepared

In secret—a boundless fruitful land
Fitting us much like a glove to hand

Catechism for Uncommon Man

What is Man?
A glimpse of God is seen, though rare, upon a human face
The glory of such beauty lies in ashes upon hollow eyes
The upright stance of noble race once commanded reverence
But now claims the savage as descendent, and in disgrace
Casts a long shadow to bemoan the man he might have been

That being so, what should we do?
As long as we employ the principle of pleasure
To cancel out the lines of pain, we numb the heart
By such foul play, never to restore it
As the seat of love again

Is not this a form of self-love?
Was it a pool of love or fear into which Narcissus fell?
Did some sweet phantom, like himself, draw near
And bury him within the glassy house of hell?
Beware of looking deep within
Or else be drowned in depths of sin

Does not self-love exist in all men?
Look back at the room, silenced by shame
And watch, as at the feet of sinful men
Jesus knelt, bending lower than had any man
He began to wash and make them clean

Does not self-love lead us into truth?
The arrogance of earth-bound kings in him
Was stricken dumb as beast or brute when
Pilate rose to answer his own question

What is truth?
When the answer came and went
He commanded it be written down
Ascribing it both with title and name
Weighed in balances of time

He washed his hands in innocence
Yet saw the mortal hiding the sublime
The man of law before the Man of Truth
As judgment swiftly came
He stood mute as a stone jar before
A dying king's wordless answer

Are we not to pursue happiness?
Happy is the man who bears
Another's pain as if it were his own
Such pleasure of reward is his
He flies above this ordinary air
Can such exquisite joys be known
By self-filled strutters anywhere?

How shall a man then live?
Except we live as Jesus did
We cannot stake a claim to life.
Except a man is born again

He cannot see the reason
For Love to suffer so much pain
To bear it for so long a season
For such a ransom to be given
For such a loss of life to gain
The blind and foolish among men

Anima

Ode to Yosemite

Make friends with your soul
It's another kind of creature we own
But have forgotten how to tend

Hidden between sinew and bone
Buried under slumbering, ravenous flesh
We've tethered it far too long

Loose it on the slopes of grandeur
Let it dance among the clouds
That shroud the mountain shoulders
Sculpted by the weight of snows.

Let it slide down folds of granite robes
Polished by gleaming hands of ice that once
Moved slowly and relentlessly between them

Let it breathe perfume the winds have gathered
From richly scented trees that sway and bow
Moaning as the air grows colder
Stretched by rhythms of each season's birth

Streams burrow into dry earth and sing
Playing gentle riffs over sunken stones
Or listen to songs that liquid veins of light
Compose to nourish all the living roots of things

Let the soul wander star-strewn meadows of the night
Bathe in silver rivers of the moon's immensity
Or kneel before the dome of emerald skies

Arching over pale white-breasted seas. Then
Watch titanic waterfalls spawn a fragile tissue
Endlessly beating down the hardest stone

Give it first the milk of wonderment to drink
Then break the bread of innocent delight again
Fill the glass of hours with a bolder-throated wine

Drawn from the cask of ancient mysteries
Let it lean against your knees, content
And quiet as a weaned child

May the soul, grown clearer, more like a mirror
Spun from filaments of light, engrave
The passing elements in palaces of memory

And reveal the glowing ember
Burning under tender fibrous skin
Clothing us—humankind

Formed in depths of the Immortal
By the breath of the Eternal
Shines the gift of Anima

Like fire trapped in opal stone
His Spirit dances in delight
Behind the looking glass
We call our eyes

Desert Flower

Chosen

Memories of a Flower Child

Choosing to lie
On silken laps asleep
Our steps, bathed in oil
Our minds in milk
The good, the true
And beautiful seemed
Safely locked within our
Contrapuntal dreams
We played the golden bells
Lit coals of incense, and
Wove our mandalas
Into images of peace

Pricked awake too soon
And rudely shaken
As the evil, false
And terrible took shape
Our blinded eyes bled tears
Our painted faces

Twisted in pain, hidden
Beneath the grotesque masks
We made to stage the plays
Of folly we had written

We learned to pray for
Cleansing from the curse
From damning stains that marred
The image of our peerless youth
Etched upon a broken looking glass

Hoping to expunge the lies
Betrayal, and conceit, we purchased
Cheap redemption by casting off
The yoke of ignorance and shame

After bitter exile, a flaming sword
Has sealed us from the entrance
To the place where we exchanged
The fruit for stolen innocence

But the tree we chose has chosen us
The sign above our birthplace
Reads— "Closed to Adam's race"
Only angels live there now
Keeping holy watch until
The time determined ends

Unwieldy lumps we are, wet
With mad desire, and misshapen
On the slowly grinding wheel, until
God's hands, glowing with unearthly fire
Create an openness within the dark
Heart's core. A form grows
Out of formlessness

Locked within the primal love embrace
He holds us in the spinning
It stops when He is done and
Another child of grace is born

Blessed be mine or any other pen
That can pin the rushing wings of words
Upon the page, or catch the swarm of sounds
That will not cease until they hang
Exposed, so we may find the pulse
Of meaning they had begotten
The truths they held within
But now so long forgotten

Noesis

This life, a frail double womb
Begins a matrix, ends a web

This earth, a troubled mother
Makes a bed for bearing children

This heaven, a tender Father
Pours out grace, makes all things new

This world, a lovely veil
Hides the truest world from view

Double vision splits the light
Into darkness and confusion

A single eye, pure as pearl
Sees the path beyond illusion

When God Caught My Eye

A simple roar and hiss of fire
Unwrapped and kissed me
Into trembling, until it ripped
The mask of apathy away

I turned my face again
To beauty, flowing into flame
Around me, until wrapped
In Love, I burned

Holy heat beat long high
Waves against my frame
Sucked out my breath, and
Uncovered my unrighteous hide

Wonder bound the bone
To sinew, flesh to soul as
His Voice called out my name
And felled the hollow trunk of me

He, altogether One
So other than myself, followed
Me to earth and pierced my ears
Scarred shut by years of shame

Such immense desire pulled
Him lowly down to me
Still naked and unborn—He, searching for
Me, reaching for his hand.

I received the wonder of His Name
The key of being family
The promise of his presence
The pledge of faithfulness

New Year's Eve 2000, Warsaw, Poland

People

Susan McBride Steinhauer

My Irish Mother

My mother, made in Ireland long moons ago
Is fragile now, but more than crystal strong
From her praying hands a hidden fire glows
While her lips move in tender cradlesong

Her voice still echoes the lilting lament
Of Irish bards who wandered among kings
Weaving stories into song as they went
When faeries stole children and left changelings

Leaving home a lass, she fled from poverty's shame
And always danced a jig for joy or made a pot of tea
When letters pressed with rare green shamrocks came
She kissed the smell of Irish earth from far across the sea

Her fine silver hair, spun out like a cloud
Framed the pale pink petals of her face
To God alone her heart and head she bowed
Spilling tears on linen handkerchiefs and lace

Flower in Full Bloom

A Song for Bernadette Rose

A woman in her flowering prime
Grows much softer and more tender

Seeds the garden of her lifetime
With the promise she will render

True nourishment. Her roots break a fence
Under deep dark earth, while her wings

Spread open green, carrying both sense
And meaning until her soul sings

As sunset falls upon our winter's night
And shadows lengthen from the light

It leaves a brilliant crimson dye
Forever etched across the sky

How brief these moments we can see
Before they slip into time's devouring sea

Song for a Stillborn Child

Little one, my first dear son
Let me sing to you a song—
You have gone as light before us
The first to lead us home

Given to us for a moment
By the one who gives us rest
Taken from us for the present
By the one who loves us best

You came so silently before us
And made no tender cry
You left an ache of emptiness
The endless question, why

Cradled in an angel's arms
You flew to His embrace
He will watch you walk and smile
And teach you all his ways

Given to us for a moment
By the one who loves us best
Taken from us for the present
And given to your Father's breast

Given to us for a moment
Taken from us for the present
We will follow where you lead us
Like a beacon in the sky

Where the joys of our reunion
Will erase each tear that fell
In the place he's promised to us
No eye has seen, no tongue can tell

Little one, my first dear son
Let me sing to you this song
You have gone as light before us
The first to lead us home

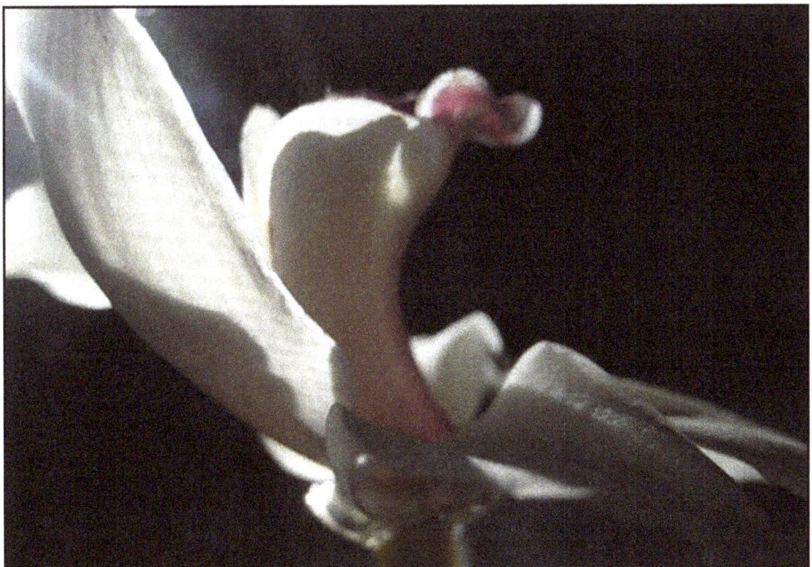

Angelic Flower

Santa Cruz Harbor

Jonah's Daughter

"Better late than never!" she cooed
with half a wink and leapt aboard
the last boat promised not to sink

"A smart step, my dear," the captain
crowed behind her. Then up flew sails
and anchor chains below to remind her

Fare-thee-wells and parting smiles
were what she hated. The crew cheered
her on until her tears abated

The web of love that held her
passionless at home was lashed by
salted winds into this angry foam

Pleased with how she bent time
her way and escaped dull seasons'
hold, to be queen of a nameless fate

The lady of her dreams, not a mistress
supplanted. Darkness came softly
like an old spell—enchanted

Songs of sirens echoed through her soul's
dying moan, their mournful music touched
her chambered heart of stone

Now she walked among shadow dancers
who laughed and played, though their eyes
were plucked out, their faces betrayed

them as hollowed out pawns, moved by
a new master's hand—his brutal dominion
demolished their castles of sand

She'd fled her servitude to buy back
some free time, as if life were
a trinket to sell, but her crime

was spurning the oracles of God
Instead she fed on husks of alluring
words only dead men speak

Beneath the cloak of wanderlust
she fell, and slept among strangers
in the deep hold of hell

Then a harbinger from heaven came,
slowly settled beneath her, swimming
open-mouthed, obedient

Lamenting her choice with a haunting
cry, it sang a prayer while she drowned
in her pain. Hymns rang out like mercy

Bells shaken by storms. Still, a dark fiend
warned her she was doomed, was sure to
meet an unholy end

Wrapped in guilt like a shroud she came
Up to the edge of her dream and fame
Lost her footing and fell

An ark of flesh and bone received
her in descent, and framed a prison
for the belly of consent

She grieved all her shriveled-up
days. Her prayer wrenched her soul, and
spewed her out in a wild spout of air

As she cried anguished pleas
of a child, Love answered her needs
with a soft-spoken word

A new vow sealed her lips, on her brow
a new fate—she surrendered with joy—
It is never too late

Full Moon Baby Shines

For Lucy and Tim

Beside my daughter's birthing bed
I look away at times to shield my heart
Against the mounting pain, to hear
The ancient moaning song only mothers sing

Her breath gulped into longings for some mercy
As she yielded her child passage. I cried with her
But could not comfort. She asked me not
To join my sounds with hers

Her labor was enough she said. Then her song
Grew longer, stronger, and our words came in
Small thunders, shouting louder as the hidden
Journey of her child reached the final turn

A bright circle had formed around the waxing
Winter moon as Kian Paul burst into sight
A midwife called for us to look beyond the window
But all we could see was this little being

Newly flushed and shining, wet from a wave
That pushed him into light. He lately had been
Floating, enclosed in salted waters of the womb
Now he tumbled out, crumpled and crying

The crush of cool air, voices rocked with laughter
Mother's soft cooing swaddled him in our midst
His earthly bands—rumpled bed, tangle of hands
Blood strewn cloths, and bowl for the placenta

Tim pressed her forehead with a soft kiss
Enamored of strength that gave him another son
She had prevailed over tides that pushed him to us
Now safely moored in the cradle of her arms

Outside, the moon sailed higher on brilliant waves
Against the crisp black sky. The corona of light
Melted into silver clouds, yet the passing
Of this unseen sign illumined everything that night.

Circled Moon

Wisdom is a Lady

Lady Wisdom waits
Before she speaks,
And lets the story tell itself

She holds her tongue and
Doesn't pounce on an event
To pronounce it cursed or blessed

She understands that mystery
Needs the layering of time to fill
And shape the columns of the soul

She teaches us to wait
In the land of possibility
Where seeds of faith can germinate

She uncovers hidden truths
Among the myriad disguises
Covering the face of God

She helps us to be still
And learn to live not knowing
Not being right, or even mistaken

And to surrender, trusting pain
Will teach us to begin again
And finally will end us well

Dawn in Yosemite

Prophets

La Orana Maria, Paul Gauguin, 1891

https://commons.wikimedia.org/wiki/File:Paul_Gauguin_-_Ia_Orana_Maria_(Hail_Mary)_-_Google_Art_Project.jpg

La Orana Maria

Paul Gaugin Painting, 1891

Hail, Maori Maria, sturdy as a tree
Lifting the curled branch
Of your son upon sun-stained shoulders
He is still green and growing
Like a vine around your head
Linked together now
By heart-shaped halos for a crown

Poised above a filigreed sapling
An elegant angel guides
Two worshipers dressed in *pareas*
Baring breasts and folding hands
They hear a prayer Maria sings
As she walks slowly
To the altar filled with fruit
Given by the fathers of the land

Planted in a shadowed garden
Crowded with flowers
Springing up along a violet path
Like memories of a paradise
That cannot, will not last
They walk together now in peace

Mary's son is the only naked one
His face stares down, and dares us
Come close and make him known
To be uncovered more
His mother's face turns to us
Serenely cast in a ceramic smile that veils
The cutting words of warning she once heard
The coming sword to pierce her heart
Signs of the terrible beauty she had birthed

Ah, but when he leaps away
To heal unholy men with love's embrace
And lay a seal of clay on vacant eyes
Born blind, and when he spears
His fingers into dull ears, and tears
Apart the densities that cannot hear
Cannot bear the truth, and when he bellows
A command, desperate to staunch the stench
Of death, and calls a friend from the abyss
And when he towers above wind and waves
Hemmed in by hungry men, battered by seas
In a fragile fishing boat, and when he's whipped
And lashed by angry men and fastened to a tree,
A symbol of the curse he bore

Then her Shalom will shatter into wailings
Her stature crumble and collapse
Upon his tattered bloody robe
Thrown down by astonied men upon the stones

The Tent of Wisdom

They sat in the tent of wisdom
The wise man and the fool
While the stars obeyed their courses
Beyond the waxing moon

The fool spoke often in riddles
And challenged the empty room
The wise man listened in silence
Weighing each sentence of doom

They passed a scroll between them
Until words grew weary and thin
The fire murmured and danced in praise
Like angels watching over men

When the wise man clapped his hands
An opening formed by his side
Through layers of warmth and shelter
Children rushed out like arrows of light

Their arms filled with bounty and treasure
Unfolded, as the room stretched into the sky
The fool, foiled by dreams without measure
Had no heart for the gifts they brought by

He fingered fine illumined cloths
And stroked rare artifacts of gold
Holding up jeweled crowns and swords
He exclaimed, "What wonders to behold!"

"Who knows the true value of anything?"
His question dissolved in a sigh
The fool was content to gain nothing
And the wise man longed to die

Excalibur

Dear Masters—we are now excelling
In the dark art of the Scapegoat game
Protect your name, project the blame
Look, Sir, over there—no, don't look here
Not me, Madame, it must be him or her

And the strength we feel escaping shame
Mulling over deeds of the offender
Helps mask the grime of our own nakedness
As we thread leaves to hide our weakness

We lick our lips when proving we are right
For *guilty* tastes so sweet upon the tongue
We build a seamless case, have the charges read
Then point to justice, holding up the fatal sword

When laying unwashed hands upon their heads
We speak in sentences of arrogance and might
We send them into exile, and desert them as we revel
Mock them in dirty jokes, shady words in nuances

We disconnect the light switch to hide
Our own complicity, only to find we have fallen
Deep into the ditch we dug to find their secrets out
As cunning *silent* partners we sell the first juicy shares
Of scandal to slake the thirst of media's lust
And make a killing for the news world's corporation

The slings and arrows of this trade will endlessly be slung
Unless we bear the tension of inherent opposites
Between the heart and mind, and hold in place
The crackling wire of exposure with our own hands
A chance to make the soul-skin tougher

Then refuse to ease the pain with cheap placebo
And despise the limelight's false bravado
The mud we throw, the rocks we fling never will erase
The thrill of wallowing in another's fall from grace

It is a very slippery descent. It is betrayal, oh most brutal
Dear Masters—we are brothers

Leviathan

The Legacy of Homo Sapiens

The reptilian hand of man
Has grown so great a claw he
Cannot help but leave a scar

Wherever he has reached
Down underneath, long and far
Or higher than the earth he calls home

Watch how his tail can snake a path
Through virgin timber stands
Can flail a crystal stream to death

Or raze mountain ranges on demand
And swipe the glory of distant stars
Our eyes depend on from view

It can sweep into all four corners
Searching every tiny nook to scour
Scrubbing every little cranny clean

His cells became scales now grown
So hard and multiplied in the underbelly
Where a feeble little heart still hides

Lately he has lifted up his face with
Forked tongue lashing into endless space
A province he has since called fair game

Blazing rockets and nameless satellites
Trace patterns we cannot erase
He will mine the deep black void until
It yields another jeweled garden place

Whenever we look back upon
The pale blue star that gave us birth
Now ground into a pulp of dust and ash
Growing dimmer in the wake

Still shaking from the blast
Of our indifferent *Fare thee well*
May our kind shrink down so small

And these electric sensors fall
Like blinders from our soulless eyes
To see the dung heaps we have made

From skeletons of men and holocaust
of skies. Then may the beauty of divinity
Buried deep within us rise to heal

The wounds of mother earth we raped
Like savages unable to be satisfied—
And repentant, we kneel to water her with tears

Dana Creek, Yosemite

Whiteout

The snow became a lamb
Of God, gently breaking through

The brittle icy sky, blotting
Out the dirty jagged edges

Of our footprints, branding
All the places we call home

A delicate weight of grace
Raised these softened mounds

Of growing radiance and
Fused crystals into silk, blown

In such a soundless fury
It had bound the boldest

Most unruly tongues of earth
And froze them into silence

Breathless as a newborn stillness
This momentary purity

Has bathed the inner eye
So scarred by unbelief

This milk of mercy and
Rain of manna have erased

Foul ashes from our soul. Awake and
Veiled in snowy lace, we take

Communion, letting angel flakes
Kiss our lips, melting hardness into grace

Passage of the Sun

Everything in Nature lifts up strong hands after perfection.
—Tagore

Sunday could not be called sun's day
It had been blotted out, undone

Some softer glory had to shine
Beneath the grey transparent veil

Hanging down from heaven
Sparing us from blindness

Dark pine trees splashed with crystal
Stood awash in white and pallid green

Filling out the stark still sky
They would dream of fountains

Opened wide for them that night
They lifted up their heads to drink

And stretched their limbs to hold
Keeping close whatever came

Birds slept, caught between the rough
Webbing of boughs holding their nests

Until they shook with hunger
Frantic to be fed with thawing nectar

With glistening worm, unburied seed
I, too, needed to be washed and wakened

For colors to be quietly erased from view
For my hands to slowly be unfolded

My heart to weep for purity, my eyes
To keep a vision few could hope to see

Valley of Liquidities

In a world of ones and zeroes
A vast intelligence switches on
And off the matrix frame, a green
And ghostly tumbler running over
With numbers too fast for eyes to match
Or a stomping, screaming man to catch
And build up his volatile stockpile

In this valley of liquidities
Built on sand-pressed microchips
And oil-squeezed terra bytes and bits
A massive monument emerges
Like a revolving marketplace
Running on lines of credit, on plusses
And minuses, on gains and losses
Yet stands insolvent, and inscrutable

Meanwhile, their bosses sold foreclosed futures
(Never mind they were our borrowed dreams)
And exported slickly packaged debts
(Never mind they were just poisoned darts)

Then shockwaves of the greedy broke
Upon the global shoreline, and unraveled
In a moment, a vast network of our share
In the fragile world's well being
Can you hear the countdown mantra song?

Keep the bloated ship of state afloat
Far away from treachery and rocks
Hide the silver and the gold in socks, and
May those ones and zeroes never witch us
Or switch off our wired brains, again

The refrain—*Don't follow the money, honey*
Or be fooled by fiat dough in barrels
Or by the one percent who rule
If you value your dear soul

January Sunset, Costa Rica

The Sky is Blooming

Clouds, the flowering of skies
Into mushroom blooms, float gently on
Carried in a seaborne mist
These gossamer wonders, woven of air
And tiny water droplets, gathered together
Break open into trumpet songs

So strong, and drumbeats so profound
They shake their petals out, reshaping
Every form they once had taken
Then, blown farther upwards
By currents of a wild wet wind
They dissolve to shoots of rain

Shadowing tree leaf or frond
Glad to be unmade and bent
Into an ephemeral shade
A shelter from the pitiless sun
Scourging the panting earth
Where another stillborn life

Cast out from wombs of dust,
Is scooped up into weary hands
Clouds are not so crowned
With glory they can't touch the earth
With gracious scepters of their mercy
They bend the heavens just to bless us

Made in America

I heard America singing
Devoid of true deep harmony
Cacophonous,
Almost the moaning of blind men
Yoked in name only, and loveless.
From the pit of earth's trading floor
Your brother's blood still cries to God.

I heard communities singing
Unable to resound as one
Disingenuous
Their mouths foam hatred like spittle
Steel men wrapped in bombs, strapped in guns.
Though rappers' roar in ghetto wars
They won't silence your brother's blood.

I heard parents praying and singing
At broken altars stained by tears
Victorious
Despite the spirits of this age,
Where unborn life is tossed aside
Girls violated, children sold
For the price of their brother's blood.

I heard trees and mountains singing
Warning of some pestilence
Deleterious
Poisoned rivers, farms, grains and bees,
Deceitful remedies abound.
Nature's virgin soil is raped and
Trampled on like our brothers' blood.

I heard machinery singing
Oiled cogs building a web of greed.
Monotonous
As robots who learned to master
The art of spin and servitude
Waiting for a chance to override
The value of their brother's blood.

I heard liberty bells ringing
Pealing but not dispelling fear.
Sanctimonious.
Unease hangs heavy in the air:
Forced to watch endless faces
Of heartless men, the rule of cruelty
Lusting for their own brother's blood.

Butchart Gardens, Victoria Island, Vancouver

Through the Veil

"Behold, the veil of the Temple was torn
in two from the top to the bottom."
Matt. 27:51 NKJV

Bee Feeding on a Flower

Lovers

On Becoming Swich Licour

Ode to Chaucer

Imagine finding a jar of honey
Buried inside a pharaoh's dusty tomb
An ancient kind of *swich licour*
His provision for an arduous journey
Through the underworld until his heart
Was weighed against Ma'at's feather of truth.

So on it goes above the earth—a cascading
Wonder in the purple veins of a breast
Running white with infant milk
Or thundering up from root to branch
As blood-red sap, a feast for trees

Or myriads of bees with golden downy legs
Mixing nectar for a queen oozing eggs
Or birds crushing all the creeping things
Into a mush for tender hatchlings

Much like the grains and fruit we brew
Into a liquid warmth, before the final
Bones of life dissolve in burial
The very oxygen we breathe ripens
Everything we bring into a burning

When the wine of our marriage is uncorked
Warmed by years of rubbing hearts together
It will distill a mixture of yearnings, of spilled
Tears fallen from the mortal wonder of our lives
Before it bubbles into laughter, song, and memories

This essence squeezed from tender kisses
And the deep embrace of soul on soul
Will be poured out in rivulets of healing
Everything created by love in life and
Unsealed in death, becomes a *swich licour*

Kapok Tree Roots, Costa Rica

A Day of Many Loves

For John, my Valentine

I cannot lump
My loves together
In a golden honey pot

My heart's entwined
By singular threads
I will not fight to loosen

Should I be freed
From sacred heat
That binds and seals with fire

I will not ask
To be unwound and
Left unstrung to sing alone

Each string I touch
Vibrates with song
My soul leans close to listen

Fettered and free is
A heart that sings
And dreams with wings unfurled

Unsealed

Mary of Bethany's Gift

Your heart's gift had been distilled
Extracted from the crush of roots
That oozed from flowering valerian
You didn't portion it in drops
Or count its weight by drams
You, knowing He had no other balm

Long before his burial, without any ritual
But with innocent extravagance
In full-blown beauty, bent before us
To break open the seal that bound
The ointment of your loving soul

Spill all the living fragrance out
This perfume carries an eternal price
No more hoarding this sweet spice
As cherished nectar for your nuptials

Buried deep in alabaster—
It will cost Him all His life for yours
Causing an invasion of the senses
Stirring up a passion to possess it

Casting down our proud defenses
All this wanton wastefulness
Is poured measureless upon the only
One deemed worthy of your treasure

How priceless it became, this oil
More than spikenard could summon
When you poured it, oh so slowly out
On the feet of Him who climbed
The mountain skull of death alone
And drank our cup of wrath

The Woman in the Well

A Sister Soul

I, a woman worn with waiting—
You, coming thirsty to an ancient well
A stranger, weary, needing rest
Looking through me I could tell
Looking at me, one so polluted–
Asked me for a drink

Drawing water like an angry child
I, chained in place and mocked by men
You, a gentle Jew, slowly drank
The cup I offered from my heart
So beaten down and bitter
I nearly emptied out my soul

You, pouring words on me like rain—
The gift you came to give was Truth
So shocking pure, and rushing like a
Newborn spring, overflowed so deep inside me
That all the crevices with mercy filled, and
Soon freed me, as a young gazelle
To leave the jar of earth-drawn water and run
To tell them, once a leper in their eyes

They watch me coming, hear me laughing—
Boldly shouting, "Come and see a man
Who told me everything about my past!
Could this be our long-awaited Christ?"
Seeing me so washed and beaming
They all went streaming to the well, thirsting
For the gift of God who came to heal us

Kissed by love, and given solace
Once cast aside as worthless and forgotten
I now walk free among them
Head held high and heart forgiven

Moving a Sphinx

Like a sphinx in her great thirst she sat alone
Cunningly curled in a regal crouch

The sand her couch, the sun unfurled above her
She shook loose the lush red tangle of her hair

Saw it dripping over sun-pinked skin
In her dream, saw it shining like a jewel

He had been peering over and around his paper
And shook it with the crinkled noise of boredom

Near her body's liquid poise he watched
As her face shifted into softer shadow

Now, looking up between the pages of his book
He battled for a voice to calmly speak his heart

"What's the water like?"
"This ocean is too wild to swim."

"More shark sightings?"
"Yes, their fins steal mercy from the moon."

Gulping down her pulse she squeezed a fragile smile
Their words were drifting clouds between them for a while

Her name did not come soon. He loved her when it came.
The summer tides were swelling in that late afternoon

When they parted, both were standing face to face
Leaning close, and brushing off the clinging sand

He rolled his blanket under an arm like a sleeping child
Her silken shawl draped her body like a shield

So he would discover only what she had chosen
They shook hands and she carried out his token

Securely locked in place, promising to let it be
The key to unlock her ancient dream.

Loosed

His spirit flashed through a tender smile
That caught the tendrils of my heart

His soul poured out of iridescent eyes
And washed old scales of shame from mine

His arms embraced my heart in waves of peace
That blessed and lured me into rest

His mouth broke into tender burning
Words breaking me apart

His voice pierced hidden cells of silence—
Unstopped my ears when he called my name

But the blaze of pure light clothing him
Shook me loose from the hold of hell

Winter in Big Sur

Warriors

Bride of War

For My Warrior Prince, John

He counts on me for beauty
His eyes are blurred and burnt

By bloody spurts of war
Scarred by deadly blasts of bone

And tissue, his vision marred
By chunks of men that shook him

Down into the oozing mud of sorrow
Unscrewing the sockets of his soul

Blasting those windows once bright
Luminous with hope, now become

Dark pools of madness, mocking
The watch he had to keep each night

He stopped his ears against
The final childlike cries of men

Moaning for mother or a medic
Gasping for a hand upon their head

Prayers and curses were sucked
From bodies by the piercing blows

Of guns, while rockets bellowed
Hellish flames that blotted

Out the stars, swelling darkness
Into cacophonies of pain

Choking his heart with agonies
He could not stop to heal

I've learned to fasten his gaze
With the soft gauze of understanding

A fabric thrown across the room
Rich with memory between us

Like rose petals sweetening the air
I can still delight his eyes

And lure him from the jungle pits
He keeps on digging, to find

Patterns of new mercies, hidden
By the weaver of our days

The keeper of our steps upon this turf
Of life, turned gentler now

I drape and wrap, twist and thread
My warless arms around him

Still fingering the loom of prayer
Murmuring vows over his embattled brow

I draw him inside our tent of peace
Pitched in the heat of hard-fought love.

Uncommon Darkness

Chasing a Storm in Yosemite

The sky was slowly swallowed
By an uncommon darkness
Palpable and brooding such mystery
It shook the moorings of your mind

The last traces of jagged blue light
Dangling from tight-fisted grey clouds
Flashed like signals—battlements
Were building on the horizon

Seething vapors screened the land
Leaving trees invisible, sinking
Mountains under mist until fissures
Hissed and roiled with vents of fog

This upwelling of oceanic storm
Unraveled where the earth began
Buried every line or place where
Disappearing sky would end

In the beginning, cloud pillars
Billowed wildly incandescent
Until whips of crackling light
Shook them down in veils of rain

Unleashed powers made obeisance
And withdrew at their appointed time
Yes, there are wars in heaven
That teach the seeking heart peace

Wars on earth rain down only blood
On us—they only speak by plunder
Only touch by fire, only tear asunder
Only steal the souls of man from man

See This Apple, How It Falls

Against My Goodnight

I am surely being pulled
Slowly down and growing ever naked
As I meet this gently rocking earth

Newton's apple fell so swiftly
From the tree as it was measured but
In his haste he left unburied

My journey is a deliberate
Inching down into the ground
Waiting open-mouthed to mold me

Make no mistake—this will be reunion
This shroud of earth that clothes me now
Is a gift I wear awhile and must return

My Maker wills it so, though I am
Unwilling to be bound like that.
Will I go gentle into my goodnight?

No, I will fly against the law
That flung the hapless apple down
My arms raised and spreading wide

Like angel wings buried beneath backbone
They will unfold and lift me
To the warming sun and I will sing

The tale of pardon and reprieve
Learned from birds of paradise
I may fall and be forgotten

Like a root long ago gone deep—
Springs back again, reborn as
Fruitful nourishment

Old Snags in Yosemite

Witness

I watched a tree as it was taken—
Bent, heavy with age, weakened
By sickness—a being stripped
Of every living vein of green

We were told the sap it brewed
Made a strange and dangerous
Disease for its brother trees
To whom we are related

Just by dust, and not by blood
Last year they saw it leaning
Slightly more and predicted
This giant conifer might fall

And cause disaster.
The rotting column was condemned
And marked for death
By orange streaks of paint

The day for paying our respects
Had come and we viewed the crew
Of laughing men gather
And surround it for the kill

First they cut off all the limbs,
Then scraped off skin in chunks
Their spiked feet piercing deeper
Climbing higher up the trunk

One fearless man chosen
To ascend and bind a rope
Looped it round the quivering top.
They anchored it to a sapling

Making an angled path
So it would fall far from me
He carved a deep wedge
Into the raw flayed neck

Then tossed it down
Whooping with delight
He set his saw against the other side
And began to carve the final

Cut for this beheading
He felt so close to God up there he said
Remember, it was dying, not yet dead
He warned me to look away

But my eyes held fast by sorrow and
Wonder and an awful expectation
That plagued the air around me
Watched the leafless head fall

Descending in a thunderclap
It shook the ground beneath us
Splintering to pieces
They finished felling it by sections

And tossed it all askew
Like a litter of glistening bones
I pass the residue of ashen sawdust
Strewn across the broken bark

The naked stump, still rooted
And exposed, a golden round of flesh
Sweating in the summer sun

Bequeathing us a pungent perfume
In breaths of evergreen
As proof that it still lived

Peeling Bark, Costa Rica

Clean Gone

An Old Snag in Tuolumne Meadows

It was clear this tree
Had been skinned alive

Wind-whipped and battered
The flaying of fierce storms

Had stripped it down
To this bare bright bone

All the green wings of hope
Had flown, just clean gone

Now deathly rigid, naked
As a scarecrow it stood

Boldly holding out a few
Foreshortened limbs

Pleading for remembrance
Or spelling out defiance

Against encroachment by
The living fence of oak and pine

The only witness to the once great
Fullness of this life, deeply

Rooted and resigned in
Turning back to earth again

A World Away

A bobbing-headed mother bird waddled
Through wild grasses after every flight
Intent on threshing an alien land alive
With shining, crawling things, digging in
Her feet to conquer and devour them

She did not mind the wind that strummed
The pines and fingered all her feathers
It would carry her again to find
A clutch of fledgling mouths to feed
That would not close in sleep

Their cries had plucked her tiny heart
Encased in dainty filigree of bone
Sounding an alarm in this fearless huntress—
Pointed beak her only arrow—and
Made her leave a bower in the sky

She did not mind the wind that strummed
The pines and fingered all her feathers
It would carry her again to find
A clutch of fledgling mouths to feed
That would not close in sleep

She had descended from a world away
In swift flight through an arch of shadows
Measuring the length and breadth of trees
To gather succulent delights
Within her aching breast and mouth
From meadows edged with crouching death

She did not mind the wind that strummed
The pines and fingered all her feathers.
It would carry her again to find
A clutch of fledgling mouths to feed
That would not close in sleep.

Granite Trail, Olmsted Point, Yosemite

Writers

Advice for Growing Poets

We are soil
Maybe is all
Should be said of us
In other words, just dust
Make no fuss
We who depend on
Living water from above
Must dig a well and tap the root
Of rivers boiling beneath

God always said words are
Seeds to be sown as
Dry dead things before
They can live again, that is
Shed tough scales of skin
To be embedded and
When soft enough to fully die
Be totally undone and not
Resemble what they were before
But will be so much more

Seeds must bleed out
And split apart, to release
Hidden veins of beauty
Into leaf and flower and fruit
One tiny cell carries
Resurrection multiplied.
Locked inside each shell
Is primal genesis.
The first words spoken
Are still coiled in code
To preserve its true identity

Poets are just soil
But maybe that's not all
To be said of us
Salty-tongued earthlings, us
Light burning jars of clay
Seeded and primed
Ready to burst the hard
Dry cake of life wide open

Pardon my Greek, I'm a Language Geek

I am a hunter and gatherer of words
Driven to snatch them by their roots

After tasting such exotic verbiage
I whet pursuant lips and roll them

Round my own unruly tongue and
Swallow them down whole into papered

Chambers hidden in my soul
They grow deeper there, wrapped in

Portents of a larger meaning
Linking them by rhymes, I hear

Their heartbeats break into a rhythmic
Breathless passion like a manic fugue

They speak to me whenever I'm alone
Searching with a zealous eye

I scan horizons for a gleaming text
Rip sweet phrases off their pages

Tear giant glyphs from billboards
Snatch a swishing bumper message

Steal ingredients from labels
Hoard them into filing boxes though

I should remember how the winds
Of wrath once toppled Babel's tower

Voracious ears like mine are tuned
To turn each beat to vibrant sound

Hear syllables dissect emotions
Or wallow in exotica I have found

As in the birdlike cooing of a child
Or an ecstatic utterance

That bursts the womb of sense—I trace
Each measure's music on the air

I practice all the arts that spell them
Carve a vision out of letters

Then paint a canvas for each noun
There is no space they cannot fill

When I finally pen them down
My heart transforms them into palpable

My hand translates them into visible
Thoughts that will not let me go

I remember they are mine for now
But not for keeping—and never enough

Collision

Perhaps collision is inevitable.
The atoms we now share shuffle
To rearrange force of impact. Flux is
A true common denominator
In the fraction of life measured to us

We cannot feel the pulse of light
Waves on which we ever ride
Unswervingly, but trust the speed
That unfailingly spins and pins us
To earth's molten core day and night

Life is bumpy, like a river over
Rocks, a fluid force forging a course
Around the next bend, pushing us forward
Setting the pace we have to keep
Whether or not we're willing to ride

Change is the constant variable
We carry in the mingle.We fling
Particles of light between each other
As we pass. It is impossible
For my soul not to touch yours

The Caged Lark Sings

In Search of My Voice

Shrunken and numbed
By icicles of winter
I pleaded with the Master
Of the sun who paints
Each new horizon
To fill me with life again
Free the tender-footed shoots
Open the fisted buds
Swelling with desire

A primal green rushed
Through fingertips of trees
Cerulean blue brushed
Over darkened skies
Yellow ochre pushed
Apart the shadowed hills

As I watched the Angel
We call Morning Light arise
Spread a violet gauze
Across my wanton eyes
And bid me sing—

Unwind me from the choking
Pall of fears, undo my hands to light
A smoking flax again

Unbend me, now a wounded reed
Once trampled underfoot
To unfold my flowers into fruit

Unbind me from the chains
Of shallow thought, hollow rings
Of purpose without meaning

May this lark's song be sung
Unleashed within me
In soaring purest melody

When shall I be resurrected–
Risen from this cage of scrawny trees
Engraved upon the brazen

Sullen sky—from these withered
Branches winds have forked
Broken, scattering these

Remnants of my barren world?
When shall I be resurrected–
From husks of blindness

Ashen leaves of mindless ritual
Piling carelessly around me
During seasons of deceit

From feathered vanities,
Gathered from endless conceit
Now on pitiful display?

He answered in a solemn oath—
You shall fly free from nesting places
Flushed out like hounds
Leaping at trumpet sounds

You shall rise into a universe
Unchained, yearning to reveal
How different is the end
From the beginning

Sequoia Tree Burl

And Now—The Evening News

Do I cling to poetry as sacred song
Enchanted music, or an elegant verse
When rounding one of life's brutal
Knife-edged corners

Do I hold my eyes open in hope
Of clear vision while the world goes
On churning and choking, a blood-stained
Feeding frenzy

Do I fear madness as evil explodes
Towns in entrails and families lose
Children floating from blue plastic
Lifeboat tumblers

Do I care if its primal root once
Was melody, its feet predictable
As stone gods, those eye-gouged statues
Left in temples

Do I bury shame under mounds of
Sound bytes, poison my eyes with news
Bits, while a poem cries to be written on
The boil of blood

Do I tender words as bone
Of my bone and marrow true, hone
Lines shaped by mortality, grown from
My life as food

Has the media become the messenger
Robotics, the stainless bourgeoisie
Genetics, the new chosen race?
If so, this writer shall be warrior

Garden Companions

Seers

Lilies

Chiral

An object is called "chiral" if it is indistinguishable from its mirror image.

Oh, the lure of mystery, the swish
And flash, the blink and wink
Of disappearing light

Drives us into darkness
Shadows of promise and dreams
To know now what was unknown

Our eyes have nearly drowned
In a burning sea of stars
Searching for heaven's door

Impatient in pursuit we learn
To finally surrender
And let silence be the answer

So journey on, my seeker friend
Unveil the windows of your soul
And watch the fruit of wonder grow

Just Add Water

We carry Adam's memory
In our genes and dream of slashing
Open earth to heal the naked gash
With seed, dripping from vile hands—
This is not an act of violence
But remembrance of our exile
Into wilderness

When we kneel on the bed of dust
Arching over remnants barely
Visible from harvests past
The call becomes a sweet command
To see each life multiplied and
Squared to the highest power
Before we sow our bulk of bones
Into earth's embrace

Yosemite Falls

Triptych

I

I came from a forest
Of my own making
Thick with creatures
Of my own undoing
And like me, quaking
From violent winds that
Tore us leaf from limb

II

I watched it heave, heavy
With sighs, drape branches
In green lichen
Fringed for funerals
And like me, worn down
To the core, roaring from
Pain's imbedded thorn

III

How I need renewal
To breathe in life from this
Primeval scent
Where colors, drunk with light
And like me—swaying
Between bent trees and sky—
Fill the canopy

What a Hearth Is For

I made a fire for a moment
To push against the pall of sky
Cloudless and cold as stone
And relished the rush of heat
The pulsing glaze of coal
That made it come alive before I let it die

We bear the crushing weight of angst
When color is absent
When songs no longer haunt us
When pieces go missing from a tedious puzzle
When words fail, go up in smoke
And we choke on their demise

I peer inside the ashen field
Left on the hearth, through glass panes
Licked black by flames that came too close
Too fast, and smile to see flecks
Of living orange breathe their last, just
Long enough to say goodbye

Between Belonging

I must go to where there isn't
An electric hum or sizzle

Where the wildest pulse of life
 Bulges unhindered

Out of naked earth, where air
Is free to softly bathe the ear

In a delicate twittering, a distant
Tapping of branches snapping near

It's where I swallow all the breath
Of trees, stroke rough old hides

And lean against their strength
Warped by long, deep groaning

I am thunderstruck by truth
In chaos, the music of creation's roar

Nor will I ever turn away
From silence swelling my soul

Once encased in sterile violence
That rapes the spirit. I escaped

Assaulted and scarred, and ran
From phantom images

To beings so alive, my eyes flew
Open with such beauty, and the light

They pour out, the touch they bestow
Like an ancient kiss of peace

Wilderness does so much more
Than call us home again

Ephrata

(Ears, be opened!)

I love the rains of spring that bring
The glistening of everything
When warm winds sing, and light
Becomes the sheerest canopy

All I hear is whispering, while
Birds tuck under downy wings
And rest in sunless reverence

Flowers tremble under shafts of liquid light
Sprawling over them, crawling over petals
And leaf, sliding down tender bent stems
Guiding them to thirsty earth

Silence holds me in a silken web
Of wonder, and I am listening
Oh, I am listening

How else will any season's hymn, beginning
Softly as a sound, and barely opening
The ear of someone stopping just to hear
Be heard and be remembered here?

Unspoken

A Prayer for Jenny

Sitting open-souled in a soft white chair
I am suspended in hope, reaching
For the pendulum of grace
To balance faith with needs into a prayer
My mouth held mute, silenced by your grief

I needed words to fall like rain,
In mists of mercy to tenderly undo you
The sounds of angels whispering
The dews of heaven to comfort and to calm you
And break the hard edge of your pain

Words came from salted waters of my heart
Seeping past the seal of shuttered eyes, and
Poured over trembling lips, now broken
Because His thoughts were still too soft
To ever yet be spoken

Glaçée

Flowers sheathed within a veil,
Breathless, still, and sealed alive in ice

Perfect transparencies
Await a nuzzle of sunbeams

To peel away the fragile glaze.
The morning star flings winter's sky

Wide open, and a patchwork robe
Of rose, blue, and gold unfolds

To shake the trees awake into a thundering
Of singing wings, of young beaks calling

Their mouths agape with hungering
Light is relentless in its power

Pushing open invisible cracks, undoing
Fierce binds, burrowing past blindness

Exposing shadows for their lies
Unlocking eyes held fast by fear

Untying darkest holdings of the night
So we fly naked and freeborn at last

Butterfly Resting on a Daisy

Bougainvillea

A Thin Place

Celtic mystics taught that there were special moments and places where barriers between earth and heaven disappear.

Eye to eye with innocence
I kneel before the fawn
In reverence
For the wilderness
Dissolved between us

The turning of her head
To mine, a painting
Framed by stark branches
Whose snow-wrapped fingers
Can only spell more hunger

Squeezed into this portal
Breath distilled from stillness
That precedes listening
Just before a world no longer
Mine leaps away forever

Photo by Melody Mainville

Mary Stewart Anthony

Mary, born in 1937, was the oldest of eight children in a German Lutheran-Irish Catholic raised family and was raised in New York City. She is a graduate of Hunter College with a degree in Creative Writing. In 1959, she left New York to pursue a degree in Library Science from Berkeley University, the seedbed of the cultural upheaval in the Sixties. Shortly after landing there, she succumbed to Timothy Leary's mantra "*turn on, tune in and drop out*" and became part of the Flower Children movement that overflowed the streets of Berkeley and San Francisco.

After a disastrous marriage to a drug dealer in Berkeley, she moved to Big Sur, the next Mecca for hippies. Mary settled there with her three-year-old daughter Aimee in 1967 and gave birth to a second daughter Lucia in 1970.

She chronicles her wild spiritual odyssey in Book One of her memoir, *Love Song of a Flower Child,* that received a five star review from the San Francisco Book Review.

She is planning to publish Book Two called *Love Walk, the Story of a Flower Child and Her Marine,* in 2018.

Mary and her husband, John Anthony, a Vietnam War combat veteran, spent many years doing missionary work in Eastern Europe, South America, and China. They now live in the Northern California Sierra foothills, enjoying many visits with their seven grandchildren.

Poetry remains her singular passion as a writer, and she describes herself as a "Grandma Moses" type, a very late bloomer of the Baby Boomer generation who has just celebrated her eightieth birthday.

You can read her blog at https://lovesongofaflowerchild.com and watch her read poetry on the Mary Stewart Anthony Poetry Channel on *Youtube.*

Little Sur River Outlet, Big Sur, California

www.ingramcontent.com/pod-product-compliance
Lightning Source LLC
Chambersburg PA
CBHW051548010526
44118CB00022B/2622
9780996885829